What Is American Sign Language?

by Gail Herman

illustrated by Robert Squier

Penguin Workshop

To Sonja, for your interest and support here, and your friendship always—GH

PENGUIN WORKSHOP
An imprint of Penguin Random House LLC
1745 Broadway, New York, NY 10019
penguinrandomhouse.com

Library of Congress Cataloging-in-Publication Data is available.

First published in the United States of America by Penguin Workshop, 2026

Manufactured in the United States of America
CJKW

ISBN 9798217049288 (paperback)
10 9 8 7 6 5 4 3 2 1

ISBN 9798217049295 (library binding)
10 9 8 7 6 5 4 3 2 1

The authorized representative in the EU for product safety and compliance is Penguin Random House Ireland, Morrison Chambers, 32 Nassau Street, Dublin D02 YH68, Ireland, https://eu-contact.penguin.ie.

Contents

What Is American Sign Language? 1
Reading the Signs 7
Signing Through the Centuries 17
Everyone Here Signed 24
Home and Abroad 30
A Language Grows 40
Slavery and Segregation 54
The War of Methods 59
Surprise Findings 70
Separate Paths, Different Languages 74
ASL Takes a Bow 81
The Good and the Bad 87
What About Now? 96
Timelines 106
Bibliography 108

What Is American Sign Language?

The year was 1894. It was football season, and schools across the United States were cheering for their teams. At Gallaudet College (say: GAL-uh-det) in Washington, DC, quarterback Paul Hubbard led the team.

Hubbard wasn't known for being physical. One coach called him "frail," adding, "I never saw Hubbard come into contact with an opponent or dive at a fumble." But Hubbard had a feel for the game.

Back then, quarterbacks called plays, just like they do today. They told the team the plan, and it had to be kept secret. Players would stand far away from their opponents, so only their teammates could hear the quarterback speaking.

Players on the Gallaudet team, though, couldn't hear. It was the first college in the world for people who were deaf or hard of hearing. Everyone at Gallaudet used American Sign Language (ASL).

Usually, Hubbard called plays from anywhere he wanted on the field. Other teams wouldn't understand ASL. This year was different. Gallaudet was playing two deaf schools. Those players could read Hubbard's signs from one end of the stadium to the other.

Then Hubbard had an idea.

Gallaudet had an "A team," Hubbard and the best players. There was a "B team," too. At practice, the teams would play each other. Of course everyone signed. So, at every scrimmage, Hubbard called his players into a circle. They kept their backs to the B team. Nobody could see their hands; nobody would know their plan.

Why not do the same when they played deaf teams? Hubbard must have wondered. Why risk the other team knowing—or stealing!—their plays?

At those games, Hubbard had his players form a ring. Maybe he used the sign for tackle, one hand held in a fist with the pointer and middle fingers pointing down, and the other hand reaching out to grab them. Or maybe Hubbard wanted a rush play, where he'd run with the ball. He could have signed that by quickly sliding one fist across the flat open palm of his other hand.

Whatever the calls, Hubbard's plays worked. Gallaudet beat the Pennsylvania School for the Deaf 24–0 and the New York School for the Deaf 20–6. In fact, Gallaudet lost only one game that entire season!

As the for the team circle? It became known as "the huddle."

After college, Hubbard started the football program at the Kansas School for the Deaf. The idea of the huddle spread to deaf schools throughout the Midwest, then even farther. Today, every team, from youth leagues to the NFL, uses the huddle. American Sign Language changed the game.

Over time, ASL has worked its way into everyday life, too. People pose for photos using the "I love you" sign. Teachers might ask students to use the ASL form of clapping: raised hands and wiggling fingers.

For people who are deaf, ASL is the way they speak and listen. It allows them to be understood. It's the foundation of an entire culture.

And it's a language like no other.

CHAPTER 1
Reading the Signs

Language is how people communicate. It's the way they express ideas, thoughts, and emotions. Language gives names to objects. Around the world, there are hundreds of spoken languages. The same is true for sign languages. There is not just one. Even if countries have the same spoken language, like Britain and the United States, each has its own way of signing.

American Sign Language
for the word *time*

British Sign Language
for the word *time*

D or *d*?

When the word *deaf* is spelled with a capital *D*, it describes someone who identifies as part of the Deaf community, a group that shares a common language, values, and experiences; maybe someone whose first language is ASL. Lowercase *d* usually refers to the medical condition of total hearing loss. People who have some hearing loss are described as hard of hearing.

American Sign Language for *Deaf* or *deaf*

Why? Signs are rooted in culture and daily life.

Different sign languages do have things in common. They all use handshapes, with hands and fingers moving into certain positions. Facial expressions are important, but even those may change from culture to culture. Frowning might show the signer is upset or unhappy. Raised eyebrows can mean the signer is confused or asking a question. Big movements could be like an exclamation point at the end of a sentence—as if the signer is raising their voice or shouting.

Asking "Why?" in ASL

Many languages use the space around the signer, along with quick or slow motions, to get ideas across. If an object is close by? The signer keeps their hands near their body. If it's in the distance? The signer moves their hands farther away. What if the signer is describing an action—like driving fast? Their movements would be quick. If the car is inching along, the signer could move slowly.

In ASL and many languages, signs are usually "iconic." That means they create a picture—or symbol—that looks like the object, idea, or action being described. For example, in ASL, the word *book* begins with hands held together, palms touching. Then the hands separate, with the pinkies still together. It looks like a book is being opened.

For *cold*, the signer makes two fists and shakes them, as if they're shivering. Then there's the other *cold*, as in when someone feels sick. It's a different sign, a movement that's like wiping a nose with a tissue.

For spoken languages that use an alphabet, every letter has its own sign, too. In ASL, some look like the written letter, like the circle-shaped *O*. When these handshapes are put together to form a word, it's called fingerspelling.

When to Spell

Spelling out a word comes in handy when the person communicating doesn't know the right sign. Some chain stores, big companies, and cities have their own signs. (One sign for Amazon copies the company's smile logo.) But names of people, small shops, or towns might need to be fingerspelled. Usually, people in the Deaf community have their own name sign, different from spelling out their given name. Community members come up with a word or phrase that describes them—maybe hair color, where they're from, or if they like to giggle.

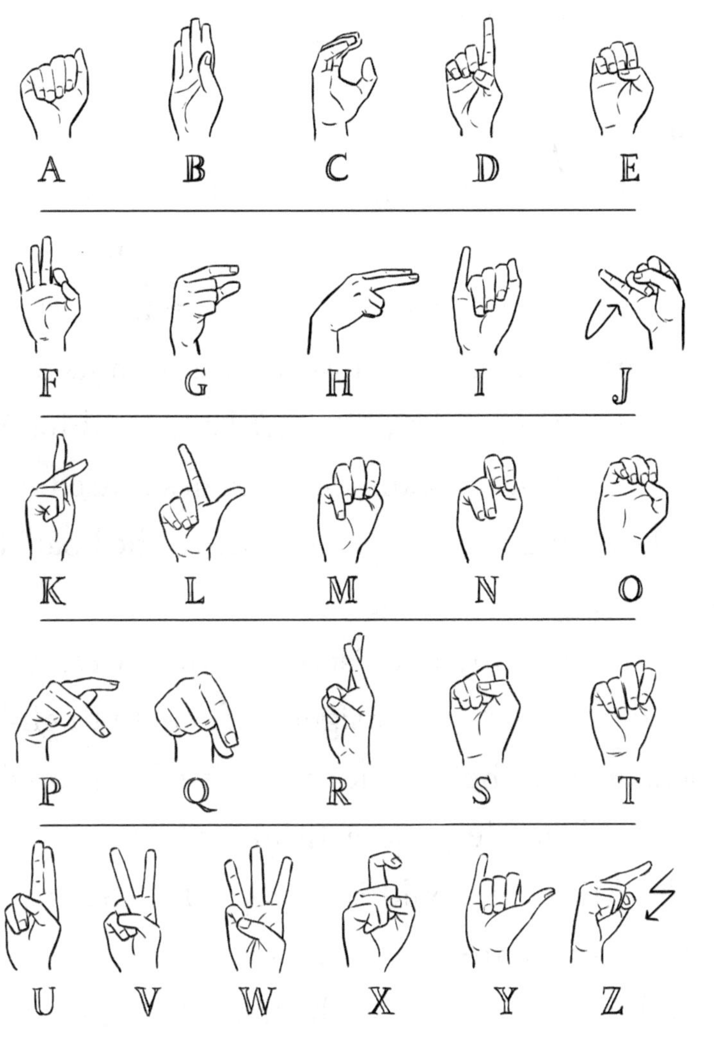
A
B
C
D
E
F
G
H
I
J
K
L
M
N
O
P
Q
R
S
T
U
V
W
X
Y
Z

ASL has its own grammar, different from other sign languages and spoken English. The sentence "Where does your family live?" may change to "Your family lives where?"

American Sign Language has its own idioms, too. Idioms are phrases that have a particular meaning when certain words are put together, different from what each word means on its own. Signing "train go sorry" doesn't have anything to do with trains. It means someone has missed out. It's like saying somebody has "missed the boat" in spoken English.

ASL has different "accents" or styles, too, depending on where the signer is from. In English, a person from the Northeast or West Coast might say "soda" to describe a drink, while someone in the Midwest would say "pop." In ASL, these differences are the accents or styles.

Take the word *pizza*, which can be signed in a number of ways. Sometimes it's just fingerspelled, but mostly everyone would understand the bouncing double *Z* shape, popular in Washington and Oregon. In California, the person may make a triangle handshape near the mouth, like a slice about to be eaten. In a diverse city like New York—where pizza is a source of pride—all three can be seen.

New Yorkers, in general, sign quickly, the same way they tend to talk. Southern signers move more slowly, and the West Coast style falls somewhere in between, with a relaxed style all its own.

Like all languages, sign languages change. Signs develop over time, as people share new experiences. The sign for *telephone* has transformed again and again because phones have changed—from needing two hands to make a call, to now, when someone just holds a cell phone up to one ear.

Changes in signing, though, go back much further than the invention of the telephone. Experts believe sign language history begins with the earliest humans.

CHAPTER 2
Signing Through the Centuries

Scientists believe early humans began to evolve between six and seven million years ago, and experts agree that deaf people were most likely present during every stage. We don't know much about these humans, but it's likely that before they developed speech, everyone used signs. As spoken language grew, deaf people would have communicated differently from hearing people.

Written language first emerged between 3500 and 3100 BCE. The earliest written record of deafness is from Egypt in the 1500s BCE. In ancient Egypt, it's believed the deaf were treated with respect. Records from ancient Greece tell a different story.

In the mid-300s BCE, a famous Greek

philosopher named Aristotle (say: AR-uh-stot-ul) thought spoken language was necessary for any kind of learning. He believed deaf people could communicate with gestures but could not be educated. Aristotle's ideas influenced other cultures. Throughout Europe, many hearing people agreed with him—how could someone who didn't speak or hear understand the world?

Even though these beliefs were false, they were passed down through centuries. Many deaf people were treated unfairly or seen as less intelligent. In some places, deaf people couldn't go to school. They couldn't own property or vote. They had few rights.

Of course, through the ages, deaf people *did* communicate. They grew up with "home signs" created by their families. Generally, these signs were iconic or "natural" and were easily understood. Still, a shared language didn't have a chance to grow. Many people were spread too far apart, living on farms or in villages.

When cities began to form, it became easier for families with deaf members to connect. In Paris and London, for instance, deaf people found one another in public spaces—markets and churches, on the streets and in their neighborhoods. Home signs became community signs. Community signs became city signs. The language was passed from one generation to the next.

More hearing people realized deaf people could reason and learn. By the 1700s, schools for the deaf were established in Europe. Meanwhile, across the Atlantic Ocean—in what would become the United States and Canada—things were very different.

For thousands of years, Indigenous people there signed—whether they were deaf *or* hearing. Everyone called it Hand Talk, a general term for signing. In many of these Indigenous cultures, pictures were a form of storytelling—carved or painted onto rocks—and they match some signs still used today. One was a straight line with a half circle at the end. It was the Indigenous sign for water in Hand Talk—an arm held out with a cupped hand, like someone sipping water from a stream.

Different nations across the continent had different sign languages, all rooted in how their own people lived. Many shared another language,

Plains Indian Sign Language for *water*

too: Plains Indian Sign Language (PISL). They used this language to communicate with one another when they traded and held peace talks, for storytelling, and in ceremonies. By the 1800s, tens of thousands of people knew it.

The Indian Sign Language Grand Council of 1930

In September 1930, the Blackfeet Nation hosted the largest intertribal meeting ever filmed. Army general Hugh L. Scott organized the historic effort with Indigenous leaders from a dozen nations, including the Sarcee (say: SAR-see), Arapaho (say: uh-RAP-uh-hoh), Bitterroot, Blackfoot, Cheyenne (say: shy-ANN), Crow, Piegan (say: PIE-guhn), Shoshone (say: sho-SHOH-nee), and Sioux (say: soo). They all came together in Browning, Montana, now the site of the Museum of the Plains Indian. The council's goal: to preserve PISL signs with a film dictionary.

Indigenous hearing children were being sent to government-run boarding schools and forbidden to speak their own language. In deaf residential schools, Hand Talk was prohibited, too. Scott explained his fears that the language would die out, then Indigenous leaders signed their names and why they were participating. One said: "These people all use different languages. They are *all* my people." Scott died before completing the project, and PISL is now an endangered language, but the film dictionary has been preserved in the National Archives and is a vital resource.

CHAPTER 3
Everyone Here Signed

The Wampanoag (say: wamp-uh-NO-ag) people had been communicating with Europeans since the 1500s when settlers arrived in what we now call New England. The Wampanoag had been living there much longer, with ancestors going back thousands of years. Some lived on a small island off the coast of Massachusetts. They called it Noepe (say: no-EPP-ay), which means "dry land amid waters." Many of them, both hearing and deaf, used a form of what would be known as Northeast Indian Sign Language.

In the early 1600s, British colonists began building settlements on the Massachusetts mainland. Not much later, some sailed to Noepe. They called it Martha's Vineyard.

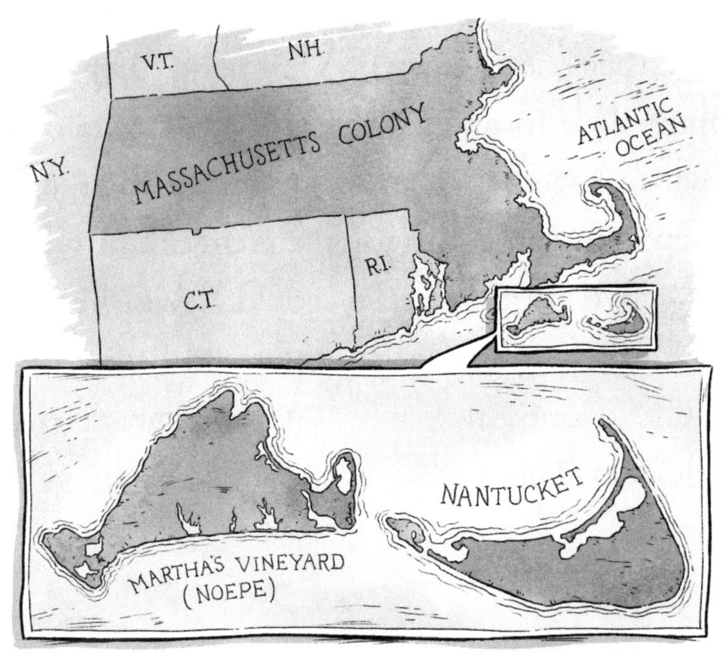

One large group of families came as a community. In England, they had lived near one another for generations, and many had an inherited trait for deafness. (An inherited trait means some kind of characteristic—like hair or eye color—that is passed down to children from parents, grandparents, or even great-grandparents.) Over time, these families had developed their own form of sign language.

In their new town of Chilmark, they built homes close to one another, too. Their children grew up together, married, and had their own children. A large part of their community was deaf. Two deaf parents could have hearing children. Two hearing parents could have a deaf child. No one knew why. At the time, science couldn't explain it.

At one point, one in five people from Chilmark were deaf. In a neighborhood called Squibnocket (say: SKWIB-nok-it), it was one in four. Most families had at least one deaf member. As the community grew, so did its sign language.

Back then, most Europeans settling in North America believed that deaf individuals weren't as smart or capable as hearing people. In Martha's Vineyard, things were different. Everybody communicated with a shared language. Hearing people knew their neighbors, friends, and family members could learn as well as anyone else. Sometimes people forgot who was deaf and who could hear. There was no separation between the groups. Deaf people married hearing people. They all fished and farmed, made a living, and raised families together. Deaf men voted. They held office and owned land.

One hearing man had an argument with a deaf neighbor. "She yelled at me," he said later when asked about his experience in the island community. “Come to think of it, I guess we did our yelling in sign language.”

Islanders used sign language all the time—even when everyone could hear. Often, signing was easier than speaking. Fishermen asked neighbors on other boats about that day’s catch. People signed on windy days, when they had to shout to be heard. At home, families used spyglasses to see

neighbors sign from a distance. If students had an "off-island" teacher, they could sign without getting into trouble for talking.

Life went on this way until the mid-1800s, when things began to change. Fewer and fewer people on Martha's Vineyard knew sign language. One reason for this was that deaf children were leaving the island. They were going to a new kind of school.

A school for the deaf.

CHAPTER 4
Home and Abroad

In the spring of 1814, Thomas Hopkins Gallaudet was twenty-six years old. He was going to be a minister. Would he be in charge of a church? Travel from town to town and preach? Gallaudet wasn't sure about his future. He went to his family's home in Hartford, Connecticut, to figure things out.

Alice Cogswell

Not long after, Gallaudet met Alice Cogswell. Alice was his family's nine-year-old neighbor. She was deaf and was often left out of neighborhood games. Gallaudet, who'd been a sickly child, understood how that felt.

A legend has grown about what happened next: To communicate with Alice, Gallaudet wrote *H-A-T* in the dirt. Then he pointed to his hat. Once Alice learned her first word, he taught her others. Actually, Alice already understood language. She'd been deafened at the age of two, after she'd had a fever. Most likely, she remembered some sounds and words. The Cogswell family used home signs, too, along with a form of fingerspelling. Alice even went to school with her sisters. But her father, Dr. Mason Fitch Cogswell, wanted a school for the deaf, where she'd get a full education. Back then, they didn't exist in the United States.

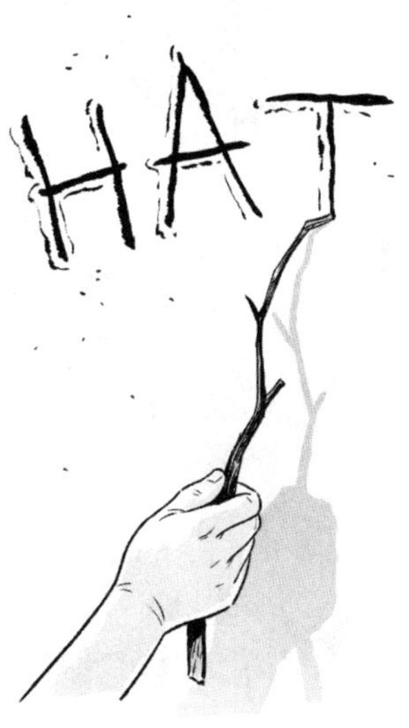

Dr. Mason Fitch Cogswell

Dr. Cogswell was a well-known surgeon. He'd researched deafness. He knew that some wealthy families sent their deaf children to the Braidwood Academy in London. The school, run by educator Thomas Braidwood and his family, focused on "oral" education. *Oral* means "spoken." While students fingerspelled, too, teachers taught them speech and lip-reading (looking at a speaker's mouth to figure out the sounds they are making).

Dr. Cogswell wanted Alice to be close to home. He did more research and found that eighty-four deaf people lived in Connecticut. Enough, he thought, to open a school in Hartford.

He formed a committee. The group decided to hire a principal and send him to London to learn the Braidwood methods. The Connecticut state government would give them money to fund a trip, and they'd ask for donations, too.

By then, Gallaudet was working with Alice. Cogswell offered him the job. Gallaudet had found his life's work: deaf education.

Gallaudet left for London in the spring of 1815. He thought it would be simple to observe classes, then come home. But the Braidwood family said Gallaudet would have to train for years. There would be long days, few breaks, and dull work.

Thomas Hopkins Gallaudet (1787–1851)

Thomas Gallaudet was born in Philadelphia, Pennsylvania, into a large, well-known family. An excellent student, he enrolled at Yale University in Connecticut at a young age, skipping a year to graduate at seventeen. After earning a second degree, he completed his religious education. Cofounder and principal at the American School for the Deaf for thirteen years, Gallaudet spent his later years lecturing on education and writing children's books and textbooks. In 1821, he married former American School student Sophia Fowler. Their eight children—all hearing—grew up using sign language. His youngest child, Edward Miner Gallaudet, would be Gallaudet University's first president.

Gallaudet tried another Braidwood school in Scotland. But staff were ordered not to share information. The Braidwoods didn't want competition. Their specific methods had to be kept secret.

Gallaudet had been away for months. Time and money were running out. Then he had another thought. Back in London, he'd seen a sign language demonstration. It was given by the Institut National de Jeunes Sourds de Paris (National Institute for the Deaf Children of Paris), the first public school for the deaf in the world.

National Institute for the Deaf Children of Paris

The school was opened in 1760 by an abbé (French priest) named Charles-Michel de L'Epée. After meeting deaf twin sisters, de L'Epée observed other deaf Parisians. He saw they had a way of communicating that helped them form bonds.

De L'Epée never considered oral training for his school. He used a different method from the Braidwood schools. Education worked best, he felt, by working with students' strengths—their ability to communicate with one another. Why have them struggle to learn speech? "Signs are the true language of the deaf," he wrote. "They speak to the eye, as speech speaks to the ear." De L'Epée learned Parisian signs, then combined them with grammar from spoken French to develop his own system. By the time Gallaudet saw the demonstration, Abbé Sicard was leading the school.

Abbé Sicard

Sicard felt as strongly as de L'Epée had about oral training. He said it was "almost always very painful, harsh . . . comparatively useless."

At the demonstration, Sicard had invited Gallaudet to visit. Now, four months later, Gallaudet was ready to see what sign language was all about.

CHAPTER 5
A Language Grows

At the Paris institute, Gallaudet spent his days learning to sign the French way. He took classes with students, had private instruction with one deaf teacher, and continued his studies with another: Laurent Clerc.

Laurent Clerc

Clerc had been a sensation at the London demonstration, answering questions on a blackboard. When asked if deaf people were unhappy because they couldn't hear, Clerc explained: "He who never had anything has never lost anything. . . . Besides, it is a great consolation . . . to replace hearing by writing and speech by signs."

Gallaudet found Clerc to be a gifted teacher with a feel for languages. Close in age, the two quickly became friends.

Gallaudet was impressed with the institute. It was clear, he thought, that signing was indeed the best way for deaf students to learn. He asked Clerc to come to Connecticut with him, keep giving him lessons, then train other teachers, too.

On the ship returning to the United States, Clerc instructed Gallaudet. In turn, Gallaudet taught Clerc written English. The two arrived in Hartford in the summer of 1816.

Laurent Clerc (1785–1869)

Laurent Clerc was born in a small village in France where his father was mayor. It's unclear if he'd been deaf from birth or had lost his hearing after falling from a high chair into a fireplace, burning his face. The accident left a scar that would become his ASL name sign. At twelve, without any education, he left home for the institute in Paris.

A brilliant student, Clerc went on to cofound the American School for the Deaf, where French signing became the foundation for ASL. Throughout his life, Clerc lectured that deaf people were equal to the hearing, and that education was key. In 1819, he married American School teacher—and former student—Eliza Boardman. They had six children.

Less than a year later, they opened the school that would be renamed the American School for the Deaf (ASD) in 1885.

Just like the Paris school, ASD was residential, which means that most students and staff lived on the grounds. Alice Cogswell was the first student to sign up. Six others followed. They ranged in age from nine to fifty. Word spread. By the end of the first year, the school had thirty-one students. It was big news across the United States. President James Monroe even paid a visit. Monroe wore a three-cornered hat, popular during the Revolutionary War. Its triangle shape became the students' sign for hat.

Already, some French signs were changing. The school was moving away from de L'Epée's system in other ways, too. De L'Epée's sentence structure followed spoken French, but English language rules proved too complicated. Instead, American signing shifted toward a grammar that felt comfortable to use; a more natural way of signing. (De L'Epée's system would eventually fade in France also, with the older, Parisian way continuing.)

At ASD, teachers didn't teach signing at all. New students picked it up from older ones—in the dorms, during meals, while doing homework. They came up with new signs and taught each other signs they used at home. Records are spotty, but it's likely that some Indigenous people studied at the school, bringing signs from their own communities, including Northeast Indian Sign Language.

In 1825, students from Martha's Vineyard

enrolled. The school's first Black student, Charles Hiller, came from Nantucket, another small Massachusetts island. More groups from the Vineyard followed, along with students from deaf communities in Maine and New Hampshire. All their signs brought changes, too.

ASD was private. Families paid for their children's education. States funded some students, as well. Local governments covered the cost for the New England groups. With a mix of backgrounds, the students' new language became a blend of cultures and signs, and their school days brought a wealth of new experiences. Each day began at 7:00 a.m. with prayer. After that came study hour, reading and writing in English, penmanship, and subjects like geography and astronomy, all taught with the help of signing. Classes didn't end until 6:00 p.m.!

Many students had never been in a classroom before. Few had been away from home. School felt like a whole new world. "I thought I was the only deaf and dumb girl in the world," one student wrote later. (In those days, *dumb* was a word for someone who didn't speak.) Over the decades, many students felt the same way. School became their second home. Finally, they were in a place where they could be understood and grow.

With so many students, ASD moved to a large green space in West Hartford.

In the meantime, other schools for the deaf were opening. Some students who graduated from ASD went on to teach at newer schools. Some founded their own. Many graduates became leaders of the Deaf community. Thomas Brown of Henniker, New Hampshire, helped establish the New England Gallaudet Association of the Deaf, the model for national Deaf organizations. Abraham Lincoln signed official papers in 1864, creating the first—and at that time, only—college for the deaf: the school that would become Gallaudet College, and eventually Gallaudet University.

The language of signs spread from the 1840s through the next four decades, bringing with it a sense of community. Common experiences and language bound people together. By the late 1800s, there were more than fifty residential schools for the deaf across the country, and the number was growing. All of them used signs in the classroom. Almost half their teachers were deaf. After graduating from deaf schools, many students stayed in nearby towns. They'd made lifelong friends. They didn't want to lose that connection.

Deaf people formed social clubs and got involved in wider communities. In 1847, *The American Annals of the Deaf and Dumb* became the first publication from the Deaf community, with issues printing throughout the year. Finally, people from every state could read Deaf-related news.

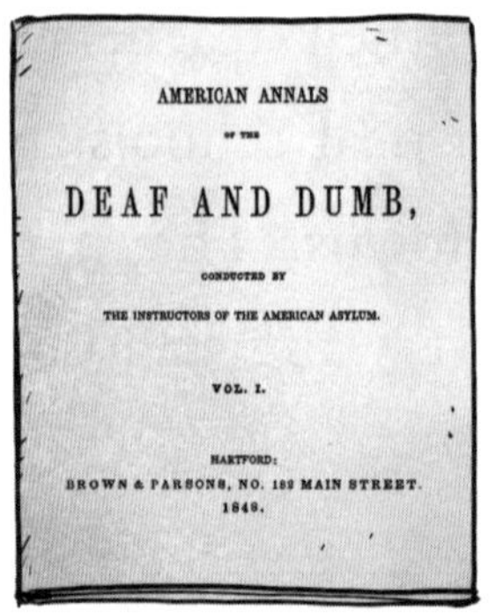

AMERICAN ANNALS

OF THE

DEAF AND DUMB,

CONDUCTED BY

THE INSTRUCTORS OF THE AMERICAN ASYLUM.

VOL. I.

HARTFORD:

BROWN & PARSONS, NO. 182 MAIN STREET.

1848.

Schools for the deaf began publishing their own newspapers, too, filled with general news, opinions, funny stories, and poems. Together they created a network called "the little paper family" for Deaf readers, their families, and allies.

Even America's favorite pastime—baseball—had a deaf connection. In the late 1800s, players from high schools for the deaf went on to the major leagues. They asked umpires to use signs: "Out," a thumbs-up handshape that moves over the shoulder. "Safe," a movement that looks like the sign for "free" with arms crossed, then straightening out to the sides. Soon umpires began to sign no matter who was playing. It helped everyone understand the calls, on the field and in the stands.

Umpires still use signs.

Signing and Deaf culture had officially come out of the classroom and into communities. It was a golden age of Deaf culture and American signing—but not for everyone.

CHAPTER 6
Slavery and Segregation

In 1619, a ship brought twenty-plus African prisoners who had been kidnapped from their homes to the colony of Virginia. Through the next two centuries, the slave trade grew, as colonists (and eventually Americans) relied on the free labor of enslaved African people and their descendants. At the time of ASD's growth, it was against the law for Black and African American people in the South to be taught to read at all.

By the mid-1800s, the United States found itself a divided nation: Slavery had been made illegal in the North. In the South, it was still the base of farming and business. In 1861, war broke out between the Union (Northern states) and the Confederacy (Southern ones).

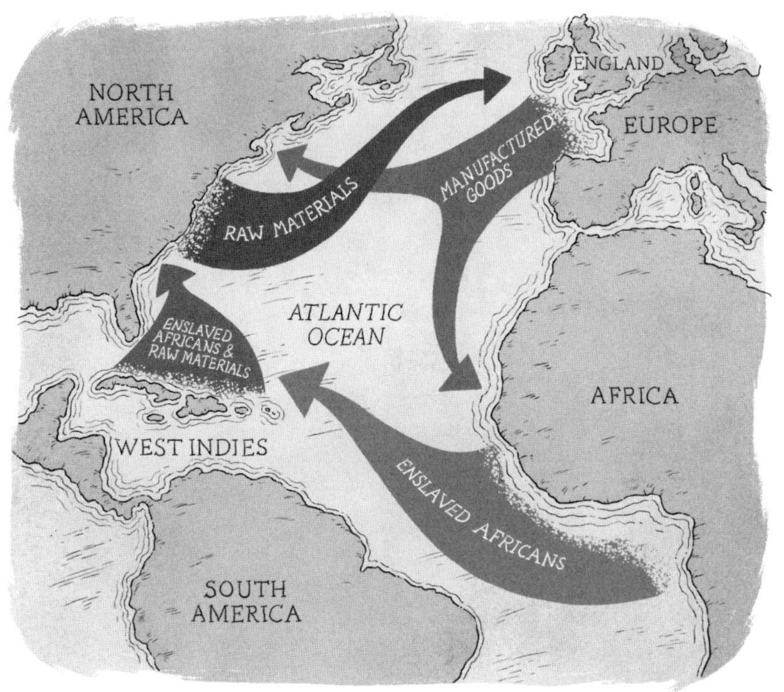

The Civil War lasted four years and ended with a Union victory. The country was reunited, and slavery was outlawed. Still, Black people faced violence, racism, and unjust laws. It was hard to find work and housing. For those who were deaf, it was even more difficult. Many were forced to stay and work on the plantations where they'd been enslaved.

Some laws *had* changed. In every state, Black children could now legally be educated. There were many schools in the South for Black children. (White and Black children were segregated, or kept apart, and educated in separate schools.) By 1870, there were tens of thousands of students enrolled. However, there was only one school for Black deaf students, which opened in 1869 in Raleigh, North Carolina. About thirteen children attended.

For the most part, Black and white students across the country didn't go to school together. In the North, even if states had made segregation illegal, many local governments got around the ruling, placing students in certain classrooms and districts, or ignoring the law outright. Then, in the 1870s, segregation became law in the Southern states. The two groups *had* to be kept apart.

More all-Black deaf schools were established in the South. Sometimes, "departments" were formed in white deaf schools. Black students lived in separate dorms. They ate in different dining halls and went to different kinds of classes and activities.

As more Black Americans migrated north, education barriers increased there, too. It was especially difficult for Black deaf children to enroll in schools. Despite its inclusive beginnings, ASD refused many Black students. They sent these students out of state to Black deaf residential schools or simply turned them away.

Many Black deaf students had to go to regular public school. There were no sign language interpreters. Teachers had no training. The children sat in classrooms, but they were unable to communicate and unable to learn. They had no one to teach them sign language, so even that was out of reach.

Decades went by with little change. But another conflict was on its way.

CHAPTER 7
The War of Methods

In 1867, two new schools for the deaf were founded, which are known today as the Clarke School in Northampton, Massachusetts, and the Lexington School in New York City. The schools were residential like ASD, but that's about all they had in common.

Rogers Hall, a dormitory at the Clarke School

At ASD and others that followed, signing was used by students and teachers to have conversations *and* to learn. It was the simplest, most direct method.

The Clarke and Lexington schools used the oral method. Students were not introduced to sign at all. In fact, signing was against the rules—anytime, anywhere.

These schools were led by hearing people who believed in speech and lip-reading. They wanted deaf children to assimilate, to become more like hearing children. They believed that sign language stood in their way.

At the time, a distrust of immigrants who spoke different languages was spreading in the United States. Many Americans believed everyone—including the deaf—should only speak English. Some feared learning ASL turned people into "foreigners among their own countrymen." Oral schools became popular.

In Europe, this "all oral" movement was already underway. In 1880, an international conference was held in Milan, Italy. Educators from all different countries went there to vote. Were they for the oral method? Or did they support sign language? The decision was almost unanimous to ban sign language in schools. More than 160 representatives voted. Only one was deaf. American representatives at the 2nd International Congress on Education of the Deaf had voted against the ban. Other American educators disagreed. Alexander Graham Bell, inventor of the telephone, became their leading voice.

Bell had been a teacher of the deaf. He was married to a deaf woman, and his mother was hard of hearing. Neither of them ever learned to sign. Both women had been born hearing, then deafened after learning spoken language. That gave them knowledge of how to form words. It made understanding speech easier, too.

Alexander Graham Bell

Bell and leading educators—all hearing—believed they knew best. Bell was famous. His beliefs held weight. He realized there were inherited traits for deafness. But the science was still incomplete. Nobody fully understood how traits passed from generation to generation. Still, people thought Bell was an expert.

Bell feared a "deaf race." He didn't want deaf people to be friends, to marry, or to have children together. Deaf culture was growing through the residential-school experience, with deaf people connecting more than ever. He thought the best way to keep that from happening was to close Deaf clubs, end Deaf newspapers, and generally keep deaf people apart. That meant stopping people from signing.

Bell's total ban on sign language didn't happen, but deaf education changed. In the early 1900s, deaf schools across the country began to include oral training. Soon it became the focus. Even ASD, where American signing began, switched to the oral method.

Many schools banned signing. In 1911, Nebraska passed a law making it illegal to teach signing. By 1919, nearly 80 percent of deaf students were taught without any signs at all. To many of their families, the oral method made sense.

Ninety percent of deaf children have hearing parents. At the time, many of those parents were told by experts that ASL would slow their child's progress or get in the way of understanding English. Decades later, research proved the opposite was true. Knowing any language makes it easier to learn another. In the meantime, damage had been done to deaf education. Deaf teachers lost their jobs to oral specialists.

Teaching with the oral method proved long and difficult. Students tried to imitate mouth and lip movements. Some were told to place their hands on their teachers' throats. They felt the vibrations made by different sounds. Then they'd touch their own, trying to make those same vocal movements. Some teachers used a stick to hold down students' tongues, pressing against the back of their throats.

Many students had to spend most of the day just working on oral skills. There was little time for subjects like math or science. They weren't allowed to sign. If they were caught, they'd be punished. Their hands might be tied together, or they might be forced to wear mittens.

Students could learn history or biology just as easily through sign language as through English. Nonetheless, if students couldn't speak well enough, they'd be called "oral failures" and made to feel bad. They'd be sent to "slower classrooms," where some signing was allowed. "Good students"—most likely those who were deafened at an older age—were rewarded. They demonstrated their skills for audiences filled with parents. But students suffered. Only 10 percent said they felt comfortable speaking or lip-reading.

There was one major exception to these policies: Black deaf schools. During segregation, Black schools generally had less money than white schools. Only certain classes were taught, like shoemaking for boys or sewing for girls. Lawmakers paid less attention to these schools. Students kept signing.

Meanwhile, Deaf leaders got together, worried about the future of sign language. They formed the National Association of the Deaf (NAD), the same year the Milan conference was held. Its founders included Edmund Booth, a graduate of ASD. Booth established the Cincinnati Day School for the Deaf and was a newspaper editor who supported sign language through the press.

In their own way, students took a stand. Even in oral schools, they kept signing. They did it outside the classroom, hiding in bathrooms, everywhere they could. Just like in the early days at ASD, older students taught younger ones, but in secret. Even though the oral method ruled in American deaf education for more than fifty years, the language remained.

CHAPTER 8
Surprise Findings

In 1955, Professor William Stokoe came to Gallaudet University to teach English. He was hearing and just starting to learn to sign. But he was fascinated by the language.

William Stokoe

At Gallaudet, Stokoe realized that students were sometimes using different signs than he'd been learning. They were using slang, an important feature of spoken language. That could be proof of something Stokoe already suspected: The American way of signing was a true language—just as complicated, just as valid, as any spoken one.

Years of research followed. Stokoe worked with two deaf colleagues. Carl Croneberg had been deafened at twelve, Dorothy Casterline at fourteen, helping them both to understand speech. They also had unusual backgrounds for Gallaudet: Croneberg was a Swedish immigrant, while Casterline was Japanese American and had grown up in Hawaii. This gave them both unique perspectives. They had a fresh way of looking at the language so they could really examine it. The three communicated with a mix of signs and spoken and written English.

Dorothy Casterline

Carl Croneberg

In 1960, Casterline, Croneberg, and Stokoe published their findings. Sign language had a grammar and sentence structure all its own. In fact, it had everything a spoken language did.

The research didn't get much notice—at Gallaudet or among language experts. But the team kept working. In 1965, they came out with a dictionary of signs. Suddenly, people paid attention. They began to think of signing in a whole new way. It wasn't just a series of gestures, the same way English wasn't just a string of spoken words.

The team's findings even took many deaf people by surprise. Their signs made up a real language, and it had a name.

American Sign Language.

Once the name appeared in the title of Casterline, Croneberg, and Stokoe's dictionary, it all became official. Recognition grew, along with acceptance among educators.

The ban on sign language began to lift.

CHAPTER 9
Separate Paths, Different Languages

The 1960s was a decade of change. Young people spoke up for peace and equality. The civil rights movement, the fight for equal rights of Black Americans, was in full swing.

What about Deaf rights? In some states, deaf people couldn't testify in court. They couldn't get a driver's license. Even voting was difficult. Black deaf people saw double discrimination. Finding work was doubly hard. Getting a good education? That was more challenging, too.

School segregation had been outlawed in 1954, but change was slow. It took years to bring Black and white students together—and it took even longer in deaf schools. The all-white main campus of the Louisiana School for the Deaf didn't enroll Black students until 1978, almost twenty-five years after the ruling.

Now, as ASL was being brought back into classrooms, schools took action. Black deaf schools began to close. Black students moved into white schools. Everything was different—even the language. How could this be, when everyone signed?

During segregation, Black adults had been kept out of white clubs, organizations, and, in the South, some public spaces. In schools *and* communities, Black and white lives had been separated. As time went on, their signing grew and changed in different ways. Black American Sign Language (BASL) developed.

BASL for the word *children*

ASL for the word *children*

Carolyn McCaskill, the director of the Center for Black Deaf Studies at Gallaudet, went to all-Black schools. Then she transferred to the Alabama School for the Deaf, a high school that had been for white students only. "I thought I signed fine," she said later. "[But] my teacher, a white woman . . . asked me outright, 'What are you signing?' I asked, 'What are *you* signing?' "

All the Black students “were lost in the classroom.” They felt “isolated” and “uncomfortable.” Slowly, things changed. “We’d see a sign,” one student said, “check in with each other to find out what it meant, and then connect it to older signs we knew. That way, when we went to school, we would know what was going on.”

Dr. McCaskill went on to study the language differences. She interviewed those Black students, now adults. She found that Black signers used more traditional ASL—more two-handed signs with big, dramatic movements. Their rhythms

Dr. Carolyn McCaskill

differed, too, with different slang words. Some signers repeated signs at the beginning and end of sentences, like they were using an exclamation point.

"Black culture is expressive," one Black adult explained. "It's all in their body language."

"I just try to be myself," another added.

The white way of signing had become the accepted form. But that didn't mean BASL wasn't as good. Dr. McCaskill's findings showed that. "Black ASL is not inferior by any means," she wrote. "It showcases the rich heritage and culture of the Black Deaf community."

CHAPTER 10
ASL Takes a Bow

There had always been Deaf artists. Deaf storytellers, too, had performed for generations in clubs and at residential schools. But in the late 1960s, different types of art grew out of ASL's growing acceptance.

Deaf artists felt freer to express themselves. Writers told more of their own stories. Poets created visual poetry, poems in motion. They

Clayton Valli became an influential ASL poet.

"rhymed" by using signs that looked alike. They gave rhythm to their words with body movement. Poetry readings weren't only for the hearing.

In 1967, the National Theatre of the Deaf (NTD) was founded. The acting company made sure to use "of the Deaf" in its name. They wanted people to know their works weren't just *for* them but *by* them, too. Deaf and hearing actors shared the stage using ASL and English. Their plays were bilingual—two-language—productions.

National Theatre of the Deaf

The NTD began in Waterford, Connecticut, with twelve actors and an idea—to create a new kind of theater. Only one person involved, founding member Bernard Bragg, had experience. Productions ranged from adaptations of Shakespeare's plays to the children's book *The Giving Tree*. Their first original work, *My Third Eye*, with castmates sharing personal stories, opened in 1971. By 2006, the group had performed in every state and on every continent.

NTD members on *Sesame Street*

An artist named Chuck Baird worked for the theater as a set painter. He was involved in a new art movement, too, with deaf artists creating pieces that focused on the Deaf experience.

These paintings could be pro Deaf rights, shows of celebration, or support for the community. Baird became "the father" of the movement, eventually called De'VIA—*De* for *Deaf*, *V* for *viewpoint*, *I* for *image*, and *A* for *art*. In his own paintings, Baird concentrated on ASL, using his hands for models.

Paintings . . . plays . . . poetry . . . They were all ways of sharing Deaf stories. The need to express the Deaf point of view was spreading—and often, it came with a big dose of humor.

Chuck Baird's painting *Whale*

Being deaf, many felt, meant you had to laugh at hearing people—and your own experiences. In the 1960s, comedians and Deaf performers signed jokes like this: "Why did the deaf man bring a flashlight to the party? He wanted to see the music."

Students joking around in their dorms told riddles like this: "Question: What is half of zero? Answer: One hundred." Why? The handshape for *zero* is the O-shape. The handshape for *C* looks like the letter *C*. But that same handshape also means "one hundred." So half a zero-shape looks like the letter *C*—one hundred!

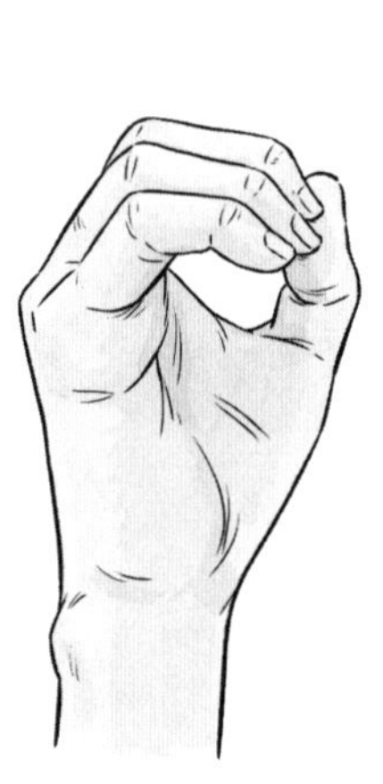

ASL for *zero*

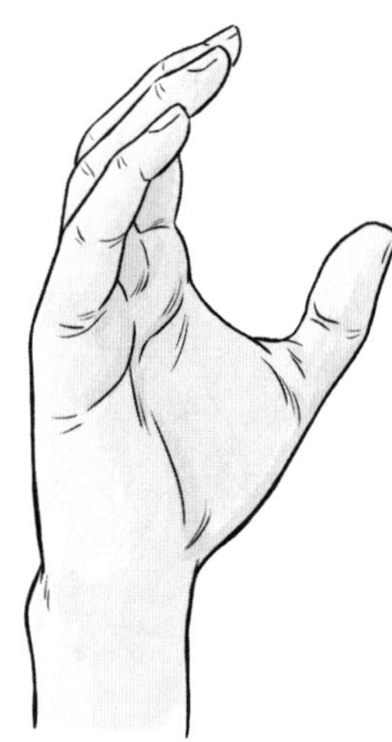

ASL for *C* and old ASL for 100

As the sixties led into the seventies and beyond, Deaf humor continued. But for deaf students, times were changing once again.

CHAPTER 11
The Good and the Bad

Beginning in the early 1970s, new communication methods were introduced in some classrooms for the deaf. These were systems, not languages—a combination of ASL and English. Signing Exact English (SEE) used English word order. Pidgin Signed English (PSE) did the same but left out words like *the* and *a*, much like sign languages do. (Today these systems are most commonly used by people whose first language is English, or native ASL signers who are communicating with a hearing person.)

Then, in 1975, a new federal law was passed. It gave students with disabilities equal opportunities in education. Students had to be placed in typical classrooms when it was suitable. The process was called mainstreaming.

President Gerald Ford signs the Individuals with Disabilities Education Act

For deaf students in public schools, everything changed. Mainstreaming meant they'd learn alongside hearing students. In most cases, nobody else in the classroom knew ASL. Many were the only deaf students in their school. Not everyone had an interpreter. And when they did, there were still challenges.

"People didn't look at me," one student said later. "They looked at the interpreter. It's like I wasn't there."

As time went on, supports grew stronger. Students could go to resource rooms with trained teachers. More public schools opened classrooms just for deaf students. Still, it seemed that hearing people were making more decisions for the deaf. To many, it didn't feel right.

In 1988, Gallaudet University turned 124 years old. Every one of its presidents had been hearing. Now it was time for the school to hire a new leader. It came down to three candidates. Two of them were deaf. This could be the change we want, students thought. A president who knows what it's like to be deaf.

The job went to a hearing woman named Elisabeth Zinser. Not only that, she didn't know how to sign. The head of the group that hired her defended the decision.

Elisabeth Zinser

Quickly, students took action. For over a week, they held protests and rallies, marching through the streets of Washington. They boycotted classes. Professors joined the cause, refusing to teach. The school closed down.

Local papers picked up the story, then the national and international press and TV stations. Interest grew, and so did support. Everyone knew what was at stake.

Four days after Zinser was named president, she resigned. Three days after that, Dr. I. King Jordan, a Gallaudet professor, became the first deaf president of the university. He led the school for almost twenty years.

The "Deaf President Now" protest worked. It raised awareness around the world: the deaf could determine their own future. As King had said, "The only thing the deaf can't do is hear"—and having the right communication tools can make the difference.

Dr. I. King Jordan

A bill was passed to ensure deaf people could call all departments, offices, and agencies of the federal government on the phone and be able to communicate. In 1990, a new equal rights bill was signed into law, the Americans with Disabilities Act (ADA). It protected people with disabilities against discrimination for jobs, housing, and education. It opened public spaces for everyday activities. Ramps were installed for those in wheelchairs. Doctors and hospitals had to provide interpreters for deaf people.

With guarantees that interpreters would be at schools, more deaf students went to college. They had greater job opportunities, with supports and assistive devices placed at offices.

Examples of hearing aids

Other assistive devices—like hearing aids and cochlear implants that are surgically placed inside the ear—are tools, too. They allow deaf people easier communication in a hearing world. But using them doesn't take away the feeling of Deaf pride. To many, being deaf isn't a disability. It's a difference—another way of experiencing the world. Some would say it's "a deaf gain" not a "hearing loss." As a deaf scientist at the University of Rochester School of Medicine told a reporter, "[Deafness] truly enriches your life."

A cochlear implant

Writer Sara Novic agrees. "[It] presents some barriers, of course," she wrote in a newspaper article. "But for me, deafness has been an overwhelmingly positive part of my life. Not a problem that needs a 'fix.'" Novic calls ASL "a beautiful language." Maybe that's why its use keeps growing.

CHAPTER 12
What About Now?

About half a million people use American Sign Language throughout the United States, parts of Canada, and in other regions. The DeafBlind Community is building on its use of ASL, too.

Groundbreaking DeafBlind advocate Helen Keller

DeafBlind Communication

Beginning in the 1880s, people who couldn't hear or see drew the ASL alphabet on people's palms. In the 1960s, Tactile American Sign Language (TASL) improved on that. (*Tactile* means something that can be felt.) A DeafBlind person places their hands on the signer's hands to feel their movements.

The DeafBlind community created Pro-Tactile ASL (PTASL) in the early 2000s, using a system of taps, strokes, and drawing lines on arms, legs, shoulders, and backs to get meaning across, along with tracing shapes or maps.

The Pro-Tactile American Sign Language sign for PASL

In US colleges, ASL is one of the most popular foreign languages studied; Deaf studies departments keep growing. More and more people are learning to sign—deaf and hearing.

More in baby sign language

Hearing families use baby sign language so their littlest ones can communicate. It helps them make connections. In Newton, Massachusetts, one entire neighborhood took ASL classes, learning to sign so they'd get to know a young deaf neighbor. Deaf schools have added programs for deaf newborns and preschoolers and opened their doors to the community so hearing people can take classes, too. High schools offer ASL as a second language.

The American School for the Deaf and most deaf schools now use a bilingual approach—a two-language/two-culture education. Classes explore Deaf history, Deaf culture, and so much more.

One public school in New York City enrolls deaf *and* hearing students. Each classroom has two teachers—one hearing, one deaf. Desks are set up in a circle so everyone can see and sign.

In 2010, the group that had banned sign languages decades earlier held another meeting. The 21st International Congress of the Education of the Deaf began with an apology for its past mistake. The statement: "Sign language is a human right."

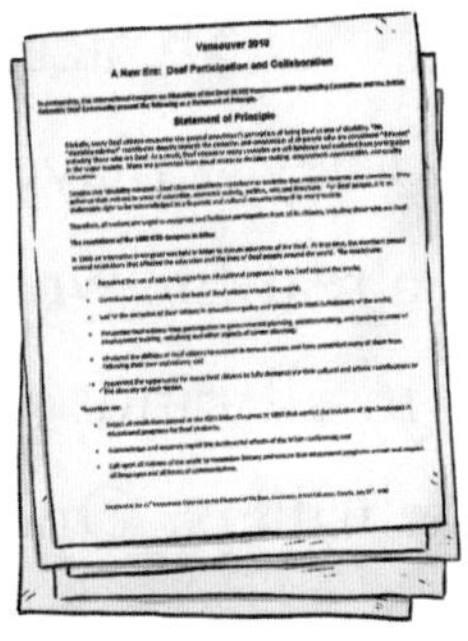
Vancouver 2010

A New Era: Deaf Participation and Collaboration

Statement of Principle

Black and Indigenous people are working to keep their sign languages alive, too. Young people are posting videos on social media, bringing awareness of BASL, Hand Talk, and American Sign Language in all its diversity.

Nakia Smith educates people about BASL on TikTok.

Deaf actors have won Academy Awards. They've played a Marvel superhero in *The Eternals*, a real-life wrestler in *The Hammer*, and have been in all kinds of movies, from family adventure to thrillers. One movie, called *CODA* ("children of deaf adults"), won Best Picture.

The cast of *CODA*

Stephanie Nogueras interprets the national anthem in ASL at Super Bowl LIX.

Super Bowl half-time and pregame shows include sign language interpreters from all backgrounds, performing alongside famous singers. Deaf athletes have played in every professional sport, including football.

25
7
53

What about college football? In 2023, the mayor of Washington, DC, declared October 21 "Home of the Huddle Day." It celebrates Paul Hubbard, Gallaudet University, and the creation of the football huddle.

Today, Gallaudet plays only hearing teams. The players don't bother going into a huddle. As Coach Chuck Golden said, "If you're going to take the time to learn sign language and interpret what we're doing in twenty-five seconds, then more power to you."

Star player and conference champion Stefan Anderson has some words for hearing people, too. "Learn some sign language. You're going to meet deaf people in your life. So be ready. It's worth it."

Timeline of American Sign Language

8000–3000 BCE	Indigenous people of the Americas begin to use Hand Talk
1694 CE	British families, carrying a trait for deafness, settle in Martha's Vineyard
1760	Abbé Charles-Michel de L'Epée formally establishes the Institut National de Jeunes Sourds de Paris
1814	Thomas Hopkins Gallaudet meets Alice Cogswell
1817	Dr. Mason Cogswell, Thomas Hopkins Gallaudet, and Laurent Clerc open the American School for the Deaf (ASD)
1864	Gallaudet University is founded
1869	The North Carolina School for the Negro Deaf and Blind, the first school for Black deaf children, opens in Raleigh
1880	The National Association for the Deaf is established to defend ASL
1965	Dorothy Casterline, Carl Croneberg, and William Stokoe publish *A Dictionary of American Sign Language on Linguistic Principles*
1967	The National Theatre of the Deaf is established
1988	Gallaudet University students rally against the hiring of a hearing president with the "Deaf President Now" protest, making worldwide news and changing people's views
2022	*CODA*, starring deaf actors Troy Kotsur and Marlee Matlin, wins the Oscar for Best Picture

Timeline of the World

8000–3000 BCE — Ancient civilizations develop in the Middle East's Fertile Crescent, establishing one of the first agricultural settlements

1694 CE — The first French dictionary is published

1760 — In Montreal on September 8, the French Army surrenders to British forces during the French and Indian War, ending French rule in Canada

1823 — Alexander Twilight, the first African American to graduate from a US college, receives his degree from Vermont's Middlebury College

1869 — The Cincinnati Red Stockings become baseball's first professional team

1880 — Wabash, Indiana, is the first US city to install electric street lights

1967 — The first handheld calculator is invented by a team of engineers at Texas Instruments

1978 — The rainbow flag—symbol of gay pride—is flown for the first time at a San Francisco parade

1988 — Table tennis is named an Olympic sport at the Seoul Korea Summer Olympics

2022 — Judge Ketanji Brown Jackson becomes the first Black woman to sit on the US Supreme Court

2023 — India overtakes China to be named the country with the largest population in the world

Bibliography

***Books for young readers**

"1930 PISL Council." Produced by General Hugh L. Scott and the US Department of the Interior, Office of Indian Affairs. Hand Talk. March 5, 2022. YouTube video, 34:30. https://www.youtube.com/watch?v=6JAq8lrRo5c.

Bayley, Robert, Ceil Lucas, and Carolyn McCaskill et al. ***The Hidden Treasure of Black ASL: Its History and Structure***. Washington, DC: Gallaudet University Press, 2011.

"Beginning American Sign Language." Miacademy Learning Channel. YouTube. https://www.youtube.com/playlist?list=PLvJNSf-7NfrMYiYROXmRTBaxGnA4BDioy.

*Bowen, Andy Russell. ***A World of Knowing: A Story about Thomas Hopkins Gallaudet***. Minneapolis, MN: Lerner, 1995.

*The Editors of Gallaudet University Press, ASL consultant Jean M. Gordon. ***The Gallaudet Children's Dictionary of American Sign Language***. Washington, DC: Gallaudet University Press, 2014.

Groce, Nora Ellen. ***Everyone Here Spoke Sign Language: Hereditary Deafness on Martha's Vineyard***. Cambridge, MA, and London: Harvard University Press, 2003.

"The Hidden History of 'Hand Talk.'" May 16, 2022. Vox. YouTube video, 10:11. https://www.youtube.com/watch?v=s1-StAlw3aE.

Tabak, John. ***Significant Gestures: A History of American Sign Language***. Westport, CT, and London: Praeger, Greenwood, 2006.

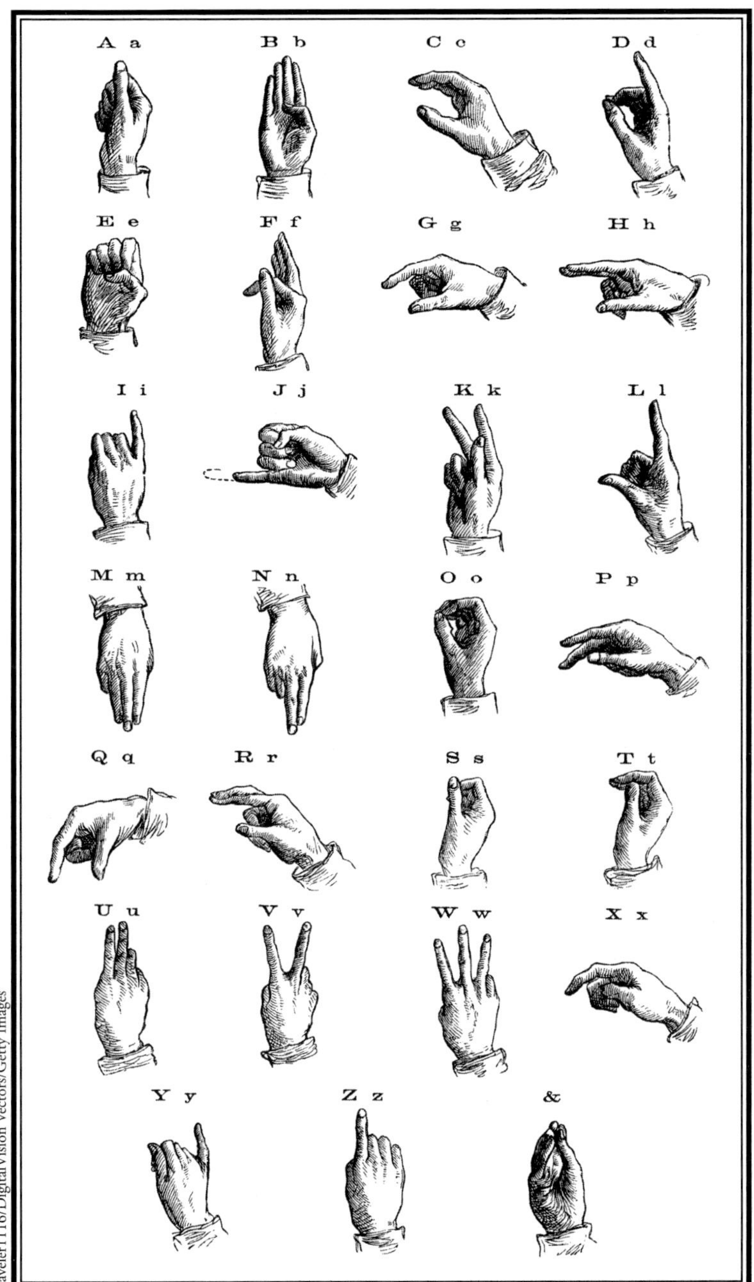

An early illustration of a sign language alphabet, 1800s

Tristan Fewings/French Select/Getty Images

Institut National de Jeunes Sourds de Paris
(National Institute for the Deaf Children of Paris)

A trading card of Abbé Charles-Michel de L'Epée

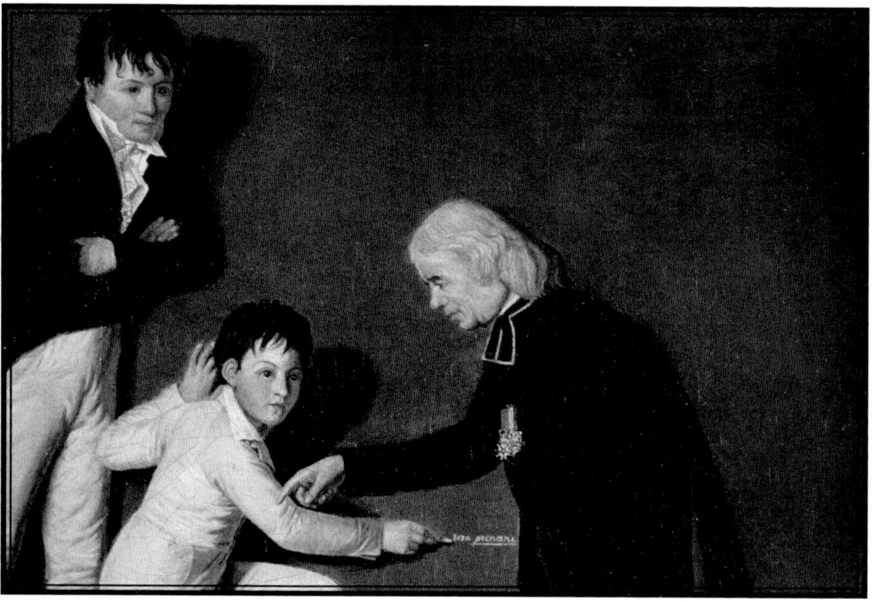

Heritage Art/Heritage Images/Hulton Archive/Getty Images

A painting of Abbé Sicard with two students

CORBIS/Corbis Historical/Getty Images

Thomas Hopkins Gallaudet (1787–1851)

Major General Hugh L. Scott, organizer of the Indian Sign Language Grand Council

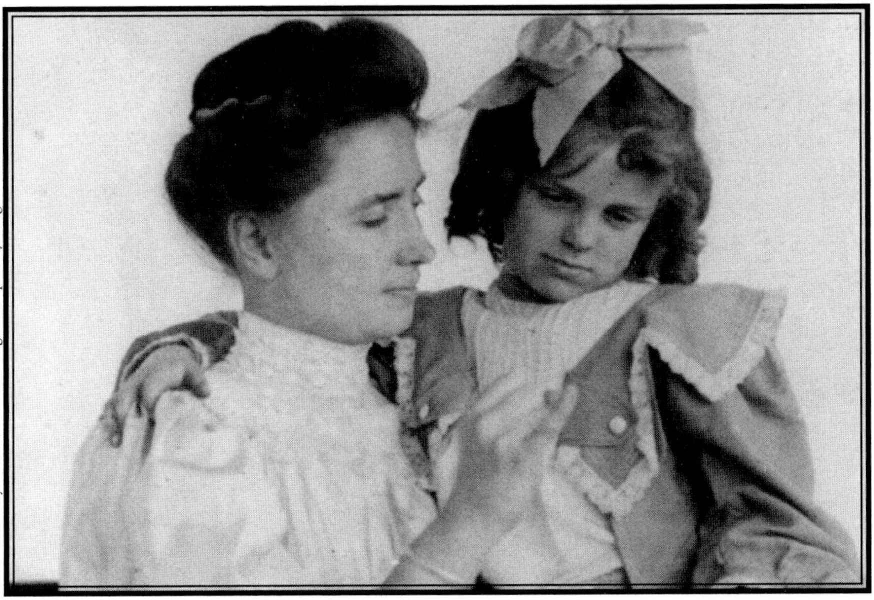

Helen Keller (left) fingerspelling with her right hand

A teacher and student at the New York School for the Deaf in White Plains

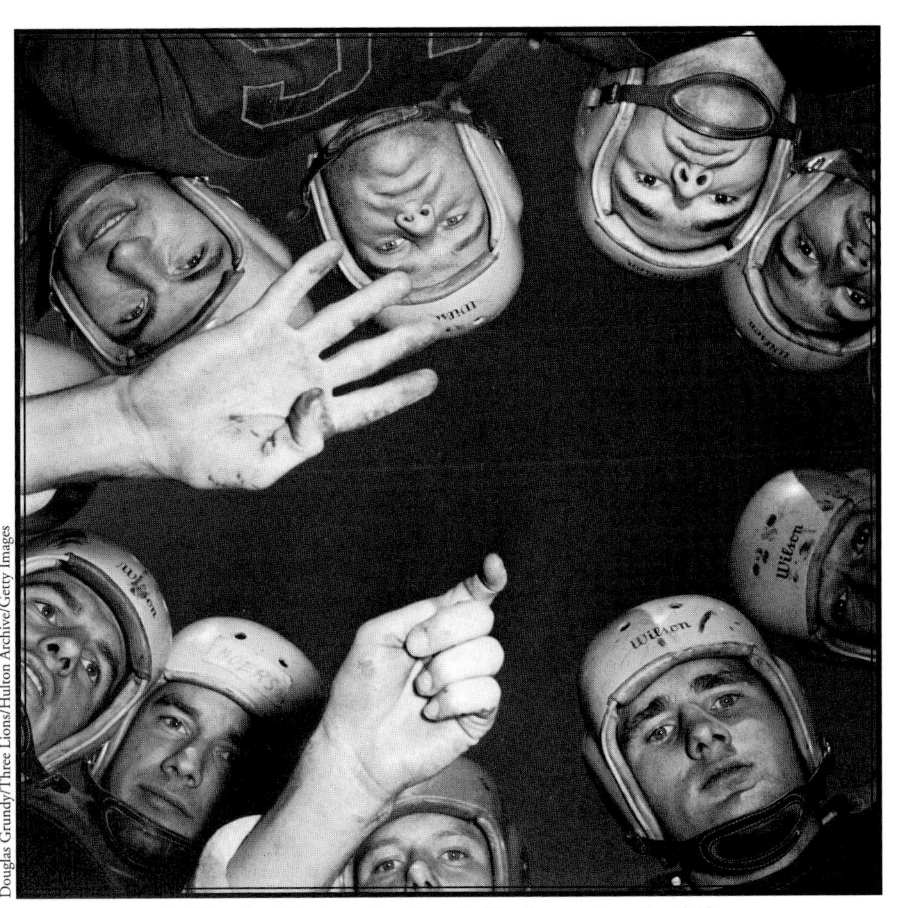

Gallaudet University football players in a huddle

Carol M. Highsmith/Buyenlarge/Archive Photos/Getty Images

Chapel Hall, Gallaudet University

Archives Department/Southern University and A&M College/HBCUs/Getty Images

Students at Southern University's state school
for deaf Black children in Louisiana

HolLynn D'Lil/Archive Photos/Getty Images

Activists speak at a 1977 rally for disability rights in the lead-up to the Americans with Disability Act

Bettmann/CORBIS/Bettmann Archive/Getty Images

Gallaudet University students during the "Deaf President Now" protests

Bettmann/Getty Images

Dr. I. King Jordan, first deaf president of Gallaudet University

Geoffrey Alfred Bagnall/Fairfax Media Archives/Getty Images

Deaf actors perform a play, 1986

John Patriquin/Portland Press Herald/Getty Images

Artist Chuck Baird with two paintings, 2004

Rodin Eckenroth/National Association of the Deaf/Getty Images Entertainment/Getty Images

The cast of *CODA* attends the National Association of the Deaf Breakthrough Awards, 2023

Bill O'Leary/The Washington Post/Getty Images

Gallaudet professor Dr. Carolyn McCaskill signs "Girl, please"

Joey McLeister/Star Tribune/Getty Images

College students learn about ASL interpreting

David Buono/Icon Sportswire/Getty Images

Otis Jones IV performs *Lift Every Voice and Sing*
in ASL at Super Bowl LIX